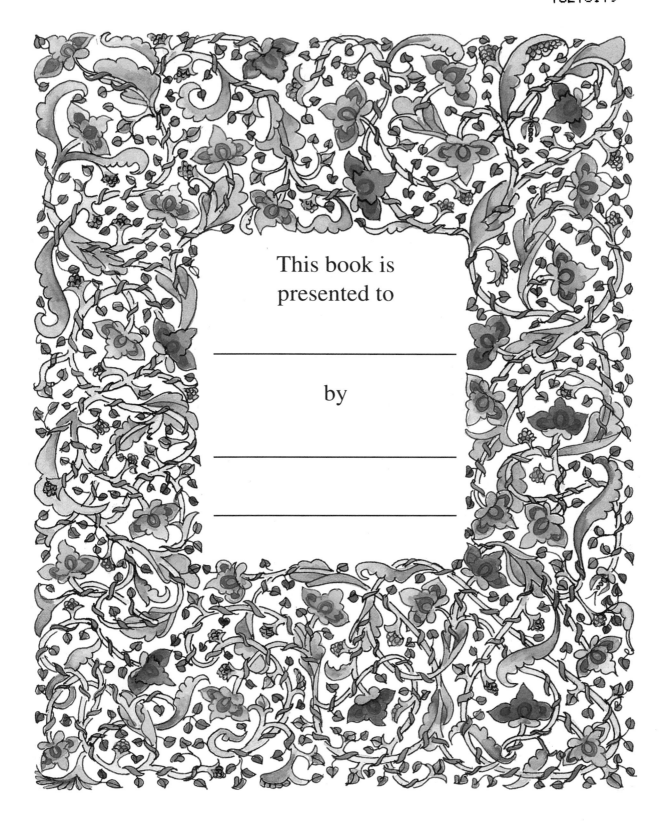

This book is
presented to

_____

by

_____

_____

My

Bar

Women of Reform Judaism/UAHC Press

New York, New York

We give thanks

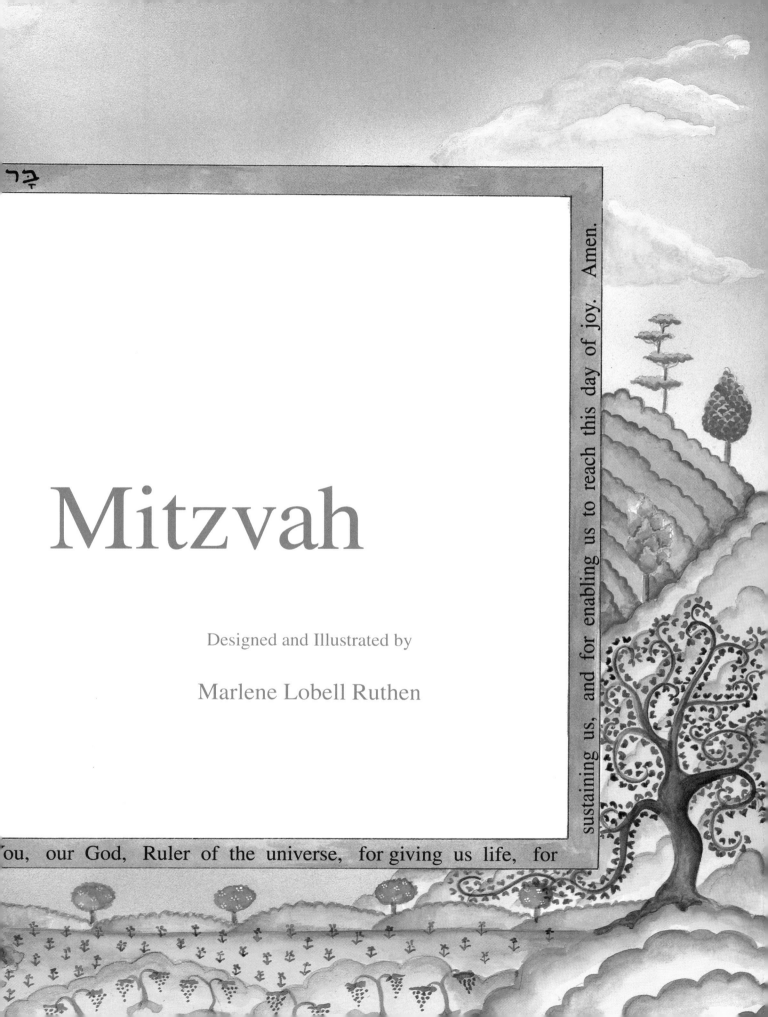

Mitzvah

Designed and Illustrated by

Marlene Lobell Ruthen

…ou, our God, Ruler of the universe, for giving us life, for sustaining us, and for enabling us to reach this day of joy. Amen.

בְּר

To Gerald
For your friendship, your encouragement, and your love

This book is printed on acid-free paper
Manufactured in the United States of America

10 9 8 7 6 5 4 3 2 1

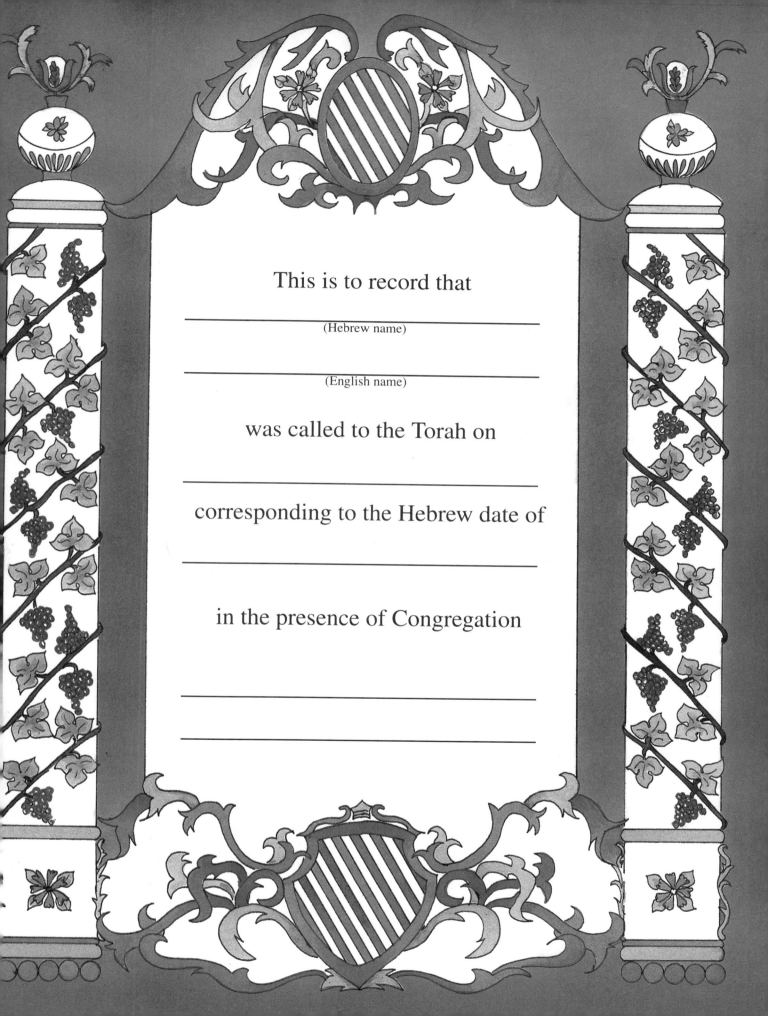

This is to record that

_____
(Hebrew name)

_____
(English name)

was called to the Torah on

_____

corresponding to the Hebrew date of

_____

in the presence of Congregation

_____

_____

Bar and Bat Mitzvah

Rabbi Daniel B. Syme

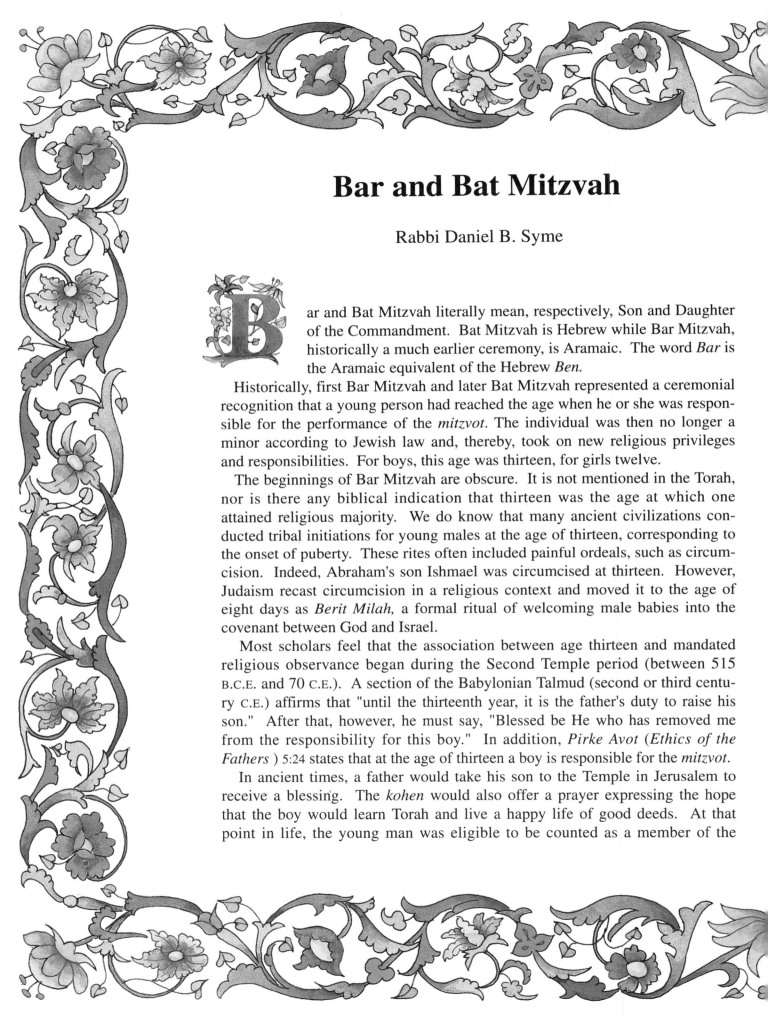

Bar and Bat Mitzvah literally mean, respectively, Son and Daughter of the Commandment. Bat Mitzvah is Hebrew while Bar Mitzvah, historically a much earlier ceremony, is Aramaic. The word *Bar* is the Aramaic equivalent of the Hebrew *Ben.*

Historically, first Bar Mitzvah and later Bat Mitzvah represented a ceremonial recognition that a young person had reached the age when he or she was responsible for the performance of the *mitzvot*. The individual was then no longer a minor according to Jewish law and, thereby, took on new religious privileges and responsibilities. For boys, this age was thirteen, for girls twelve.

The beginnings of Bar Mitzvah are obscure. It is not mentioned in the Torah, nor is there any biblical indication that thirteen was the age at which one attained religious majority. We do know that many ancient civilizations conducted tribal initiations for young males at the age of thirteen, corresponding to the onset of puberty. These rites often included painful ordeals, such as circumcision. Indeed, Abraham's son Ishmael was circumcised at thirteen. However, Judaism recast circumcision in a religious context and moved it to the age of eight days as *Berit Milah,* a formal ritual of welcoming male babies into the covenant between God and Israel.

Most scholars feel that the association between age thirteen and mandated religious observance began during the Second Temple period (between 515 B.C.E. and 70 C.E.). A section of the Babylonian Talmud (second or third century C.E.) affirms that "until the thirteenth year, it is the father's duty to raise his son." After that, however, he must say, "Blessed be He who has removed me from the responsibility for this boy." In addition, *Pirke Avot* (*Ethics of the Fathers*) 5:24 states that at the age of thirteen a boy is responsible for the *mitzvot*.

In ancient times, a father would take his son to the Temple in Jerusalem to receive a blessing. The *kohen* would also offer a prayer expressing the hope that the boy would learn Torah and live a happy life of good deeds. At that point in life, the young man was eligible to be counted as a member of the

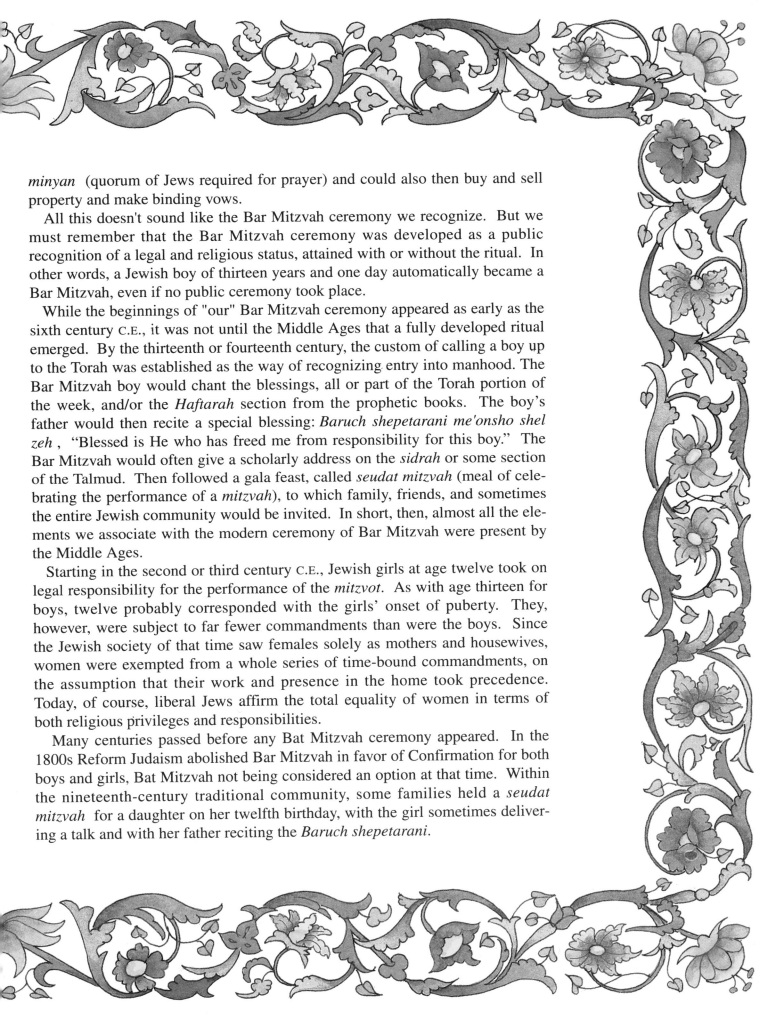

minyan (quorum of Jews required for prayer) and could also then buy and sell property and make binding vows.

All this doesn't sound like the Bar Mitzvah ceremony we recognize. But we must remember that the Bar Mitzvah ceremony was developed as a public recognition of a legal and religious status, attained with or without the ritual. In other words, a Jewish boy of thirteen years and one day automatically became a Bar Mitzvah, even if no public ceremony took place.

While the beginnings of "our" Bar Mitzvah ceremony appeared as early as the sixth century C.E., it was not until the Middle Ages that a fully developed ritual emerged. By the thirteenth or fourteenth century, the custom of calling a boy up to the Torah was established as the way of recognizing entry into manhood. The Bar Mitzvah boy would chant the blessings, all or part of the Torah portion of the week, and/or the *Haftarah* section from the prophetic books. The boy's father would then recite a special blessing: *Baruch shepetarani me'onsho shel zeh* , "Blessed is He who has freed me from responsibility for this boy." The Bar Mitzvah would often give a scholarly address on the *sidrah* or some section of the Talmud. Then followed a gala feast, called *seudat mitzvah* (meal of celebrating the performance of a *mitzvah*), to which family, friends, and sometimes the entire Jewish community would be invited. In short, then, almost all the elements we associate with the modern ceremony of Bar Mitzvah were present by the Middle Ages.

Starting in the second or third century C.E., Jewish girls at age twelve took on legal responsibility for the performance of the *mitzvot*. As with age thirteen for boys, twelve probably corresponded with the girls' onset of puberty. They, however, were subject to far fewer commandments than were the boys. Since the Jewish society of that time saw females solely as mothers and housewives, women were exempted from a whole series of time-bound commandments, on the assumption that their work and presence in the home took precedence. Today, of course, liberal Jews affirm the total equality of women in terms of both religious privileges and responsibilities.

Many centuries passed before any Bat Mitzvah ceremony appeared. In the 1800s Reform Judaism abolished Bar Mitzvah in favor of Confirmation for both boys and girls, Bat Mitzvah not being considered an option at that time. Within the nineteenth-century traditional community, some families held a *seudat mitzvah* for a daughter on her twelfth birthday, with the girl sometimes delivering a talk and with her father reciting the *Baruch shepetarani*.

The first known Bat Mitzvah in North America, that of Judith Kaplan, daughter of Mordecai Kaplan, was held in 1921. Rabbi Kaplan, founder of the Reconstructionist movement, scheduled his daughter's Bat Mitzvah on a Friday night. Judith recited the *berachah*, read her section from the *Chumash* (not the Torah scroll itself) and its English translation, and then recited the concluding *berachah*. Bat Mitzvah was born. Reform, which had by this time reintroduced Bar Mitzvah, and then Conservative congregations quickly adopted Bat Mitzvah, though in slightly different forms.

In all branches of Judaism, Bar Mitzvah is usually celebrated on the first Shabbat after the boy's thirteenth birthday. Occasionally Bar Mitzvah is marked at a somewhat later date to enable family and friends to be present.

Few, if any, Orthodox congregations have a formal ceremony of Bat Mitzvah, while Conservative congregations, where Bat Mitzvah is celebrated, may do so at either age twelve or thirteen. In Reform temples, girls, like boys, mark symbolic entry into Jewish adulthood at age thirteen.

Bar/Bat Mitzvah ceremonies are not always held on Shabbat. We recall that the public recognition of one's attaining Jewish religious majority involves being called up to the *bimah* to chant or recite the *berachot* over the Torah and/or the *berachot* before and after the *Haftarah* (a selection from the Bible's prophetic books). Since the Torah may be read on Monday, Thursday, Friday night, or Saturday morning, Bar/Bat Mitzvah celebrations are currently observed on all of these days.

In Conservative congregations, Bar Mitzvah is usually held on Shabbat morning while Bat Mitzvah is often held on Friday night. Girls may read from the Torah or, alternatively, chant the *berachot* before and after the *Haftarah,* as well as the *Haftarah* itself. In Reform temples, of course, boys and girls participate in the service in exactly the same way, according to their congregation's Bar Mitzvah or Bat Mitzvah practice.

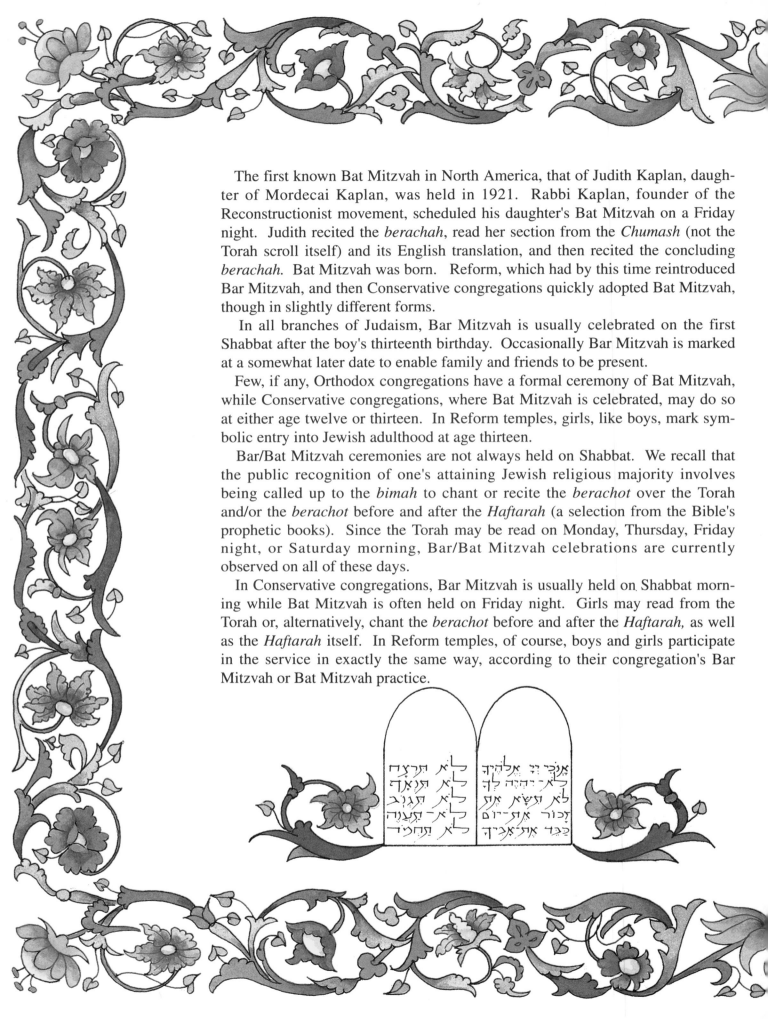

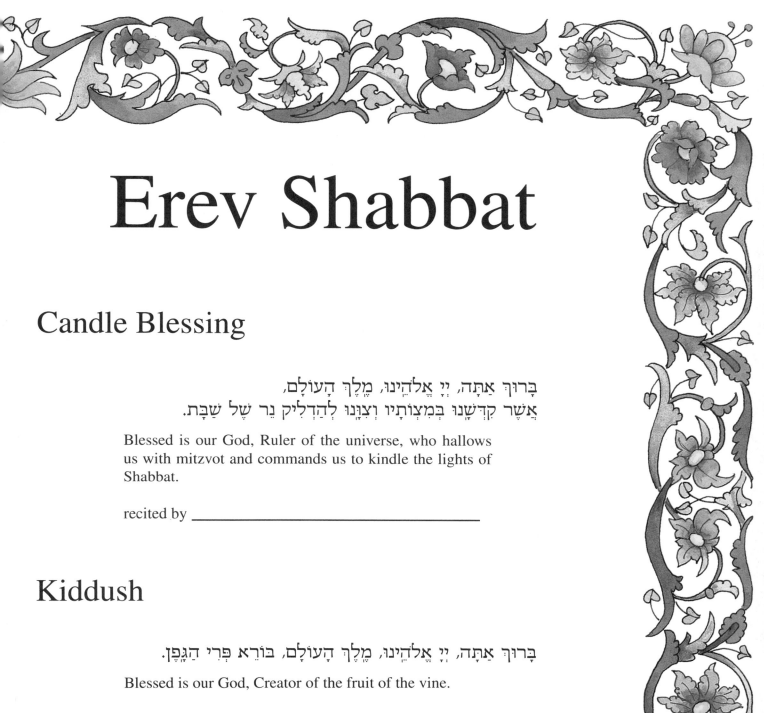

Erev Shabbat

Candle Blessing

בָּרוּךְ אַתָּה, יְיָ אֱלֹהֵינוּ, מֶלֶךְ הָעוֹלָם,
אֲשֶׁר קִדְּשָׁנוּ בְּמִצְוֹתָיו וְצִוָּנוּ לְהַדְלִיק נֵר שֶׁל שַׁבָּת.

Blessed is our God, Ruler of the universe, who hallows
us with mitzvot and commands us to kindle the lights of
Shabbat.

recited by _____

Kiddush

בָּרוּךְ אַתָּה, יְיָ אֱלֹהֵינוּ, מֶלֶךְ הָעוֹלָם, בּוֹרֵא פְּרִי הַגָּפֶן.

Blessed is our God, Creator of the fruit of the vine.

recited by _____

Oneg Shabbat

hosted by _____

Sharing In

_____
Rabbi

_____
Cantor

_____
President of the congregation

_____
President of the brotherhood

_____
President of the sisterhood

_____
Congregational representative

Bene Mitzvot

_____

_____

_____

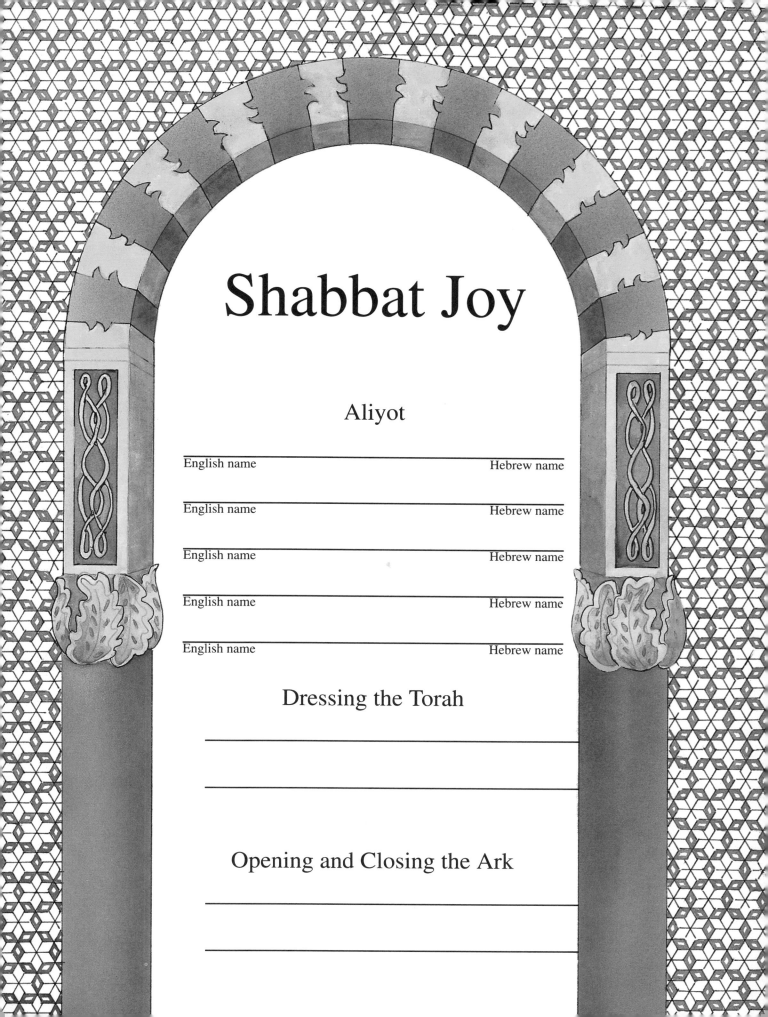

Shabbat Joy

Aliyot

English name _____ Hebrew name

English name _____ Hebrew name

English name _____ Hebrew name

English name _____ Hebrew name

English name _____ Hebrew name

Dressing the Torah

_____

_____

Opening and Closing the Ark

_____

_____

Torah Blessings

Before the Reading

בָּרְכוּ אֶת־יְיָ הַמְבֹרָךְ!
בָּרוּךְ יְיָ הַמְבֹרָךְ לְעוֹלָם וָעֶד!
בָּרוּךְ אַתָּה, יְיָ אֱלֹהֵינוּ, מֶלֶךְ הָעוֹלָם, אֲשֶׁר בָּחַר־בָּנוּ מִכָּל־הָעַמִּים
וְנָתַן־לָנוּ אֶת־תּוֹרָתוֹ. בָּרוּךְ אַתָּה, יְיָ, נוֹתֵן הַתּוֹרָה.

Praise God, to whom our praise is due.
Praised be God, to whom our praise is due now and
for ever!
Blessed is our God, Ruler of the universe, who has
chosen us from all peoples by giving us the Torah.
Blessed is God, Giver of the Torah.

After the Reading

בָּרוּךְ אַתָּה, יְיָ אֱלֹהֵינוּ, מֶלֶךְ הָעוֹלָם, אֲשֶׁר נָתַן לָנוּ תּוֹרַת
אֱמֶת וְחַיֵּי עוֹלָם נָטַע בְּתוֹכֵנוּ. בָּרוּךְ אַתָּה, יְיָ, נוֹתֵן הַתּוֹרָה.

Blessed is our God, Ruler of the universe, who has
given us a Torah of truth, implanting within us eternal
life. Blessed is God, Giver of the Torah.

Torah

Place copy of your portion in Hebrew here

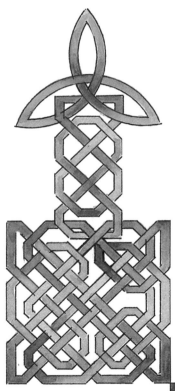

This is the Torah that Moses placed before the people of Israel to fulfill the word of God.

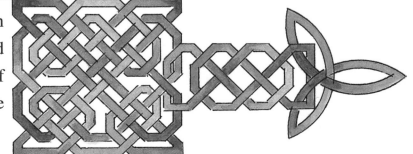

וְזֹאת הַתּוֹרָה אֲשֶׁר־
שָׂם מֹשֶׁה לִפְנֵי
בְּנֵי יִשְׂרָאֵל עַל־
פִּי יְהוָֹה בְּיַד־מֹשֶׁה.

Place copy of your portion in Hebrew here

Portion

Torah

Place copy of your portion in English here

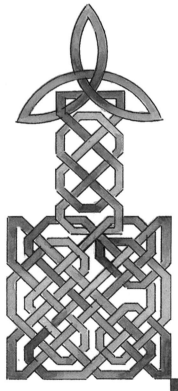

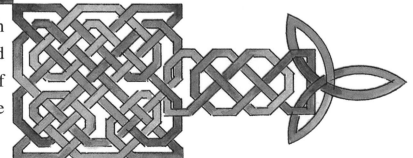

This is the Torah that Moses placed before the people of Israel to fulfill the word of God.

וְזֹאת הַתּוֹרָה אֲשֶׁר־
שָׂם מֹשֶׁה לִפְנֵי
בְּנֵי יִשְׂרָאֵל עַל־
פִּי יְהוָֹה בְּיַד־מֹשֶׁה.

Place copy of your portion in English here

Portion

Haftarah

Place copy of your portion in Hebrew here

Place copy of your portion in English here

יִהְיוּ לְרָצוֹן אִמְרֵי־פִי
וְהֶגְיוֹן לִבִּי לְפָנֶיךָ
יְיָ צוּרִי וְגוֹאֲלִי.

May the words of my mouth and
the meditations of my heart be
acceptable to You, O God, my
Rock and my Redeemer.

Prayers

My own prayer

My parents' prayer

_____

_____

_____

_____

_____

_____

_____

_____

_____

My grandparents' prayer

_____

_____

_____

_____

_____

_____

_____

Jewish

School _____

Years attended _____

Religious school principal _____

Teachers

_____ _____

_____ _____

_____ _____

_____ _____

_____ _____

Favorite Projects

_____

_____

_____

_____

Education

Special memories

_____

_____

_____

_____

_____

Preparation for This Special Day

Teachers

_____

_____

I will never forget...

_____

_____

_____

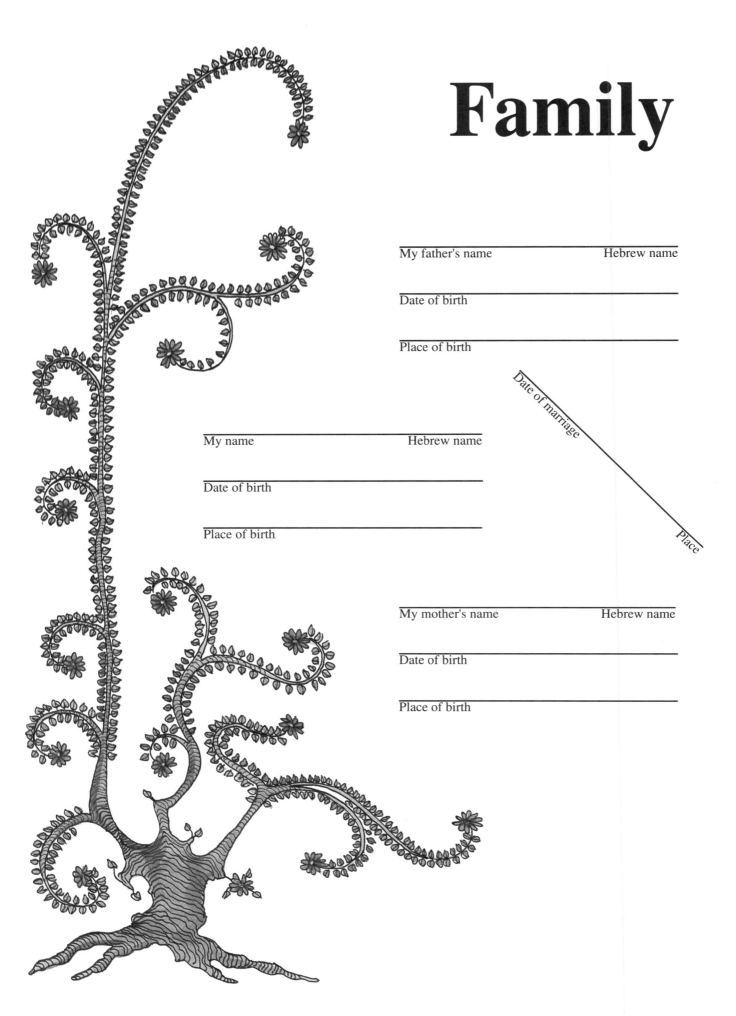

Family

My father's name   Hebrew name

Date of birth

Place of birth

Date of marriage

Place

My name   Hebrew name

Date of birth

Place of birth

My mother's name   Hebrew name

Date of birth

Place of birth

History
Father's Family

My grandfather's name _____ Hebrew name _____

Date of birth _____ Place _____

Date of marriage _____ Place _____

My grandmother's name _____ Hebrew name _____

Date of birth _____ Place _____

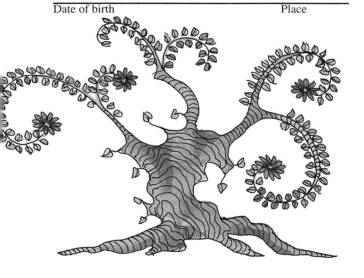

Mother's Family

My grandfather's name _____ Hebrew name _____

Date of birth _____ Place _____

Date of marriage _____ Place _____

My grandmother's name _____ Hebrew name _____

Date of birth _____ Place _____

My great-grandfather _____ Hebrew name _____

Date of birth _____ Place _____

Date of marriage _____ Place _____

My great-grandmother _____ Hebrew name _____

Date of birth _____ Place _____

My great-grandfather _____ Hebrew name _____

Date of birth _____ Place _____

Date of marriage _____ Place _____

My great-grandmother _____ Hebrew name _____

Date of birth _____ Place _____

My great-grandfather _____ Hebrew name _____

Date of birth _____ Place _____

Date of marriage _____ Place _____

My great-grandmother _____ Hebrew name _____

Date of birth _____ Place _____

My great-grandfather _____ Hebrew name _____

Date of birth _____ Place _____

Date of marriage _____ Place _____

My great-grandmother _____ Hebrew name _____

Date of birth _____ Place _____

Great-Great-

Father's Family

My great-great-grandfather   Hebrew name

Date of birth   Place

Date of marriage   Place

My great-great-grandmother   Hebrew name

Date of birth   Place

My great-great-grandfather   Hebrew name

Date of birth   Place

Date of marriage   Place

My great-great-grandmother   Hebrew name

Date of birth   Place

My great-great-grandfather   Hebrew name

Date of birth   Place

Date of marriage   Place

My great-great-grandmother   Hebrew name

Date of birth   Place

My great-great-grandfather   Hebrew name

Date of birth   Place

Date of marriage   Place

My great-great-grandmother   Hebrew name

Date of birth   Place

Grandparents
Mother's Family

My great-great-grandfather _____ Hebrew name _____

Date of birth _____ Place _____

Date of marriage _____ Place _____

My great-great-grandmother _____ Hebrew name _____

Date of birth _____ Place _____

My great-great-grandfather _____ Hebrew name _____

Date of birth _____ Place _____

Date of marriage _____ Place _____

My great-great-grandmother _____ Hebrew name _____

Date of birth _____ Place _____

My great-great-grandfather _____ Hebrew name _____

Date of birth _____ Place _____

Date of marriage _____ Place _____

My great-great-grandmother _____ Hebrew name _____

Date of birth _____ Place _____

My great-great-grandfather _____ Hebrew name _____

Date of birth _____ Place _____

Date of marriage _____ Place _____

My great-great-grandmother _____ Hebrew name _____

Date of birth _____ Place _____

My Sisters and Brothers

Name   Date of Birth
_____
_____
_____
_____
_____
_____

My Cousins

Name   Date of Birth
_____
_____
_____
_____
_____
_____
_____

My Aunts and Uncles

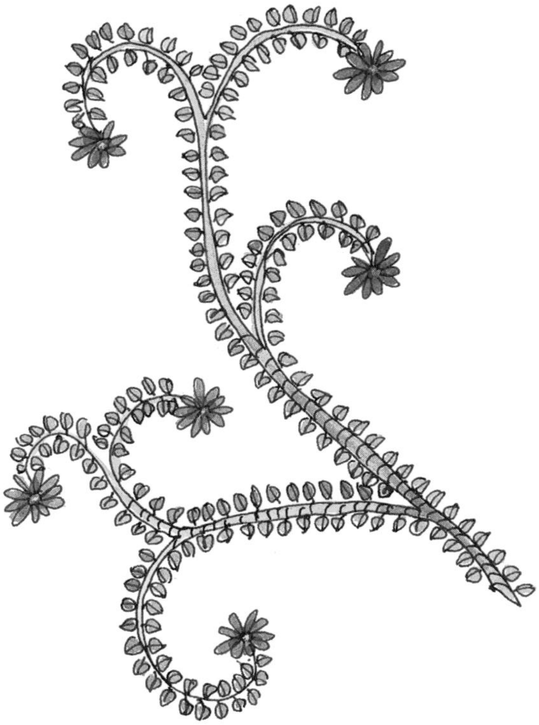

Name   Date of Birth

_____

_____

_____

_____

_____

_____

_____

My Extended Family

Name   Date of Birth

_____

_____

_____

_____

_____

_____

_____

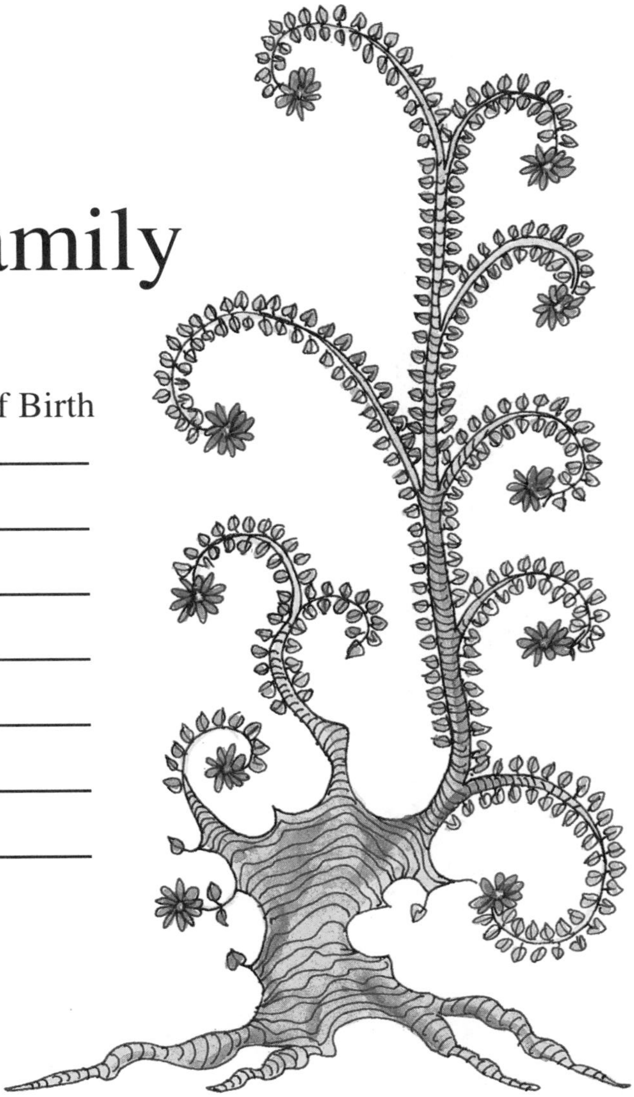

In Celebration

Paste invitation here

How We Celebrated

Special Moments

Guests

How I Felt

My Favorite Photo